Contents

Some words are shown in bold, **like this**. You can find out what they mean by looking in the glossary.

What are maps?

A map is a drawing of a part of the world. There are many kinds of maps. Some maps show things like streets and buildings or hills and mountains. They help us find our way around. Weather maps show us what the weather will be like.

4

↑ Some maps have pictures of the real-life objects we want to find.

Investigate

Mapping

Louise Spilsbury

www.raintreepublishers.co.uk
Visit our website to find out more information about Raintree books.

To order:

☎ Phone 0845 6044371

🖹 Fax +44 (0) 1865 312263

🖳 Email myorders@raintreepublishers.co.uk

Customers from outside the UK please telephone +44 1865 312262

Raintree is an imprint of Capstone Global Library Limited, a company incorporated in England and Wales having its registered office at 7 Pilgrim Street, London, EC4V 6LB - Registered company number: 6695582

Edited by Siân Smith, Charlotte Guillain, and Vaarunika Dharmapala
Designed by Joanna Hinton-Malivoire
Original illustrations © Capstone Global Library
Picture research by Elizabeth Alexander and Sally Cole
Originated by Modern Age Repro House Ltd
Printed and bound in China by Leo Paper Group

ISBN 978 0 431933 42 9 (hardback)
14 13 12 11 10
10 9 8 7 6 5 4 3 2 1

ISBN 978 0 431933 50 4 (paperback)
15 14 13 12 11
10 9 8 7 6 5 4 3 2

British Library Cataloguing in Publication Data
Spilsbury, Louise.
Mapping. – (Investigate)
526-dc22
A full catalogue record for this book is available from the British Library.

Acknowledgements
We would like to thank the following for permission to reproduce photographs: Alamy pp. **4** (© Itani Images), **21** (© Betty LaRue), **23** (© Dennis MacDonald), **29** (© Gorilla Photo Agency Ltd); Getty Images pp. **6** (Dan Callister), **20 & 30 bottom right** (Victoria Blackie); iStockphoto p. **25** (© Freeze Frame Studio); Photolibrary pp. **5** (Wave RF), **7** (Thomas Frey/imagebroker.net), **9** (Comstock/Creatas), **10** (Gonzalo Azumendi/Age Fotostock), **14** (Steve Vidler/Imagestate), **15** (Nicolas Thibaut/Photononstop), **19** (Mike Berceanu), **22** (Mike Tittel/OSF).

Cover photograph of a map of Europe on a globe reproduced with permission of Alamy/© Brownstock Inc.

Every effort has been made to contact copyright holders of material reproduced in this book. Any omissions will be rectified in subsequent printings if notice is given to the publishers.

➡️ Maps of the countryside help to stop people from getting lost.

Most maps show only things that are there all the time, like hills and houses. Maps of places do not usually show things like cars or people. Some maps, such as weather maps, show something that moves or changes.

Making maps

Maps are often made from **aerial** photographs. People take aerial photographs from an aeroplane or **satellite** that flies or hovers above the Earth. Aerial photographs show what Earth looks like from above. The mapmaker then decides what needs to be on the map.

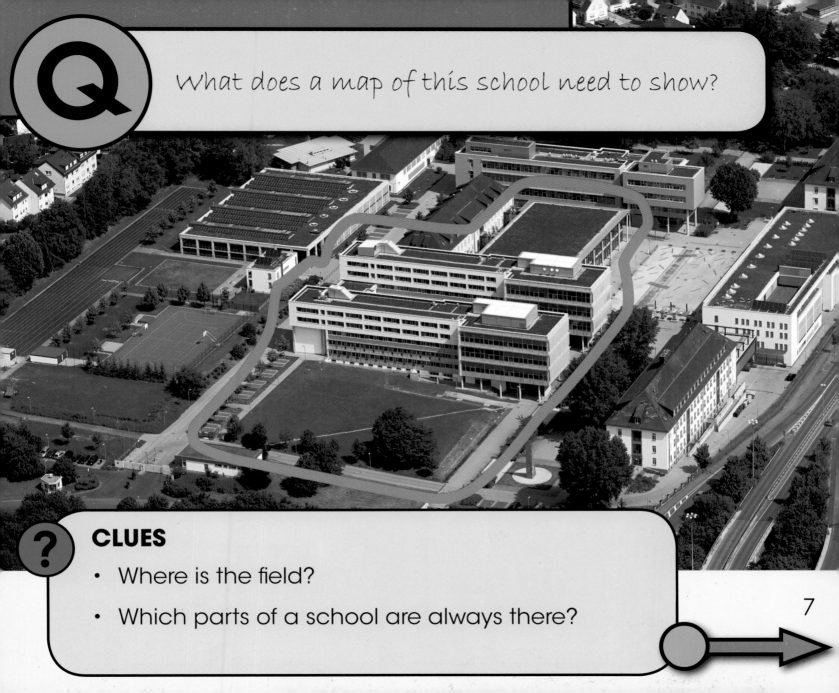

Q What does a map of this school need to show?

? CLUES

- Where is the field?

- Which parts of a school are always there?

7

A A map of a school needs to show the buildings and places that are there all the time. These are the school's **permanent** features.

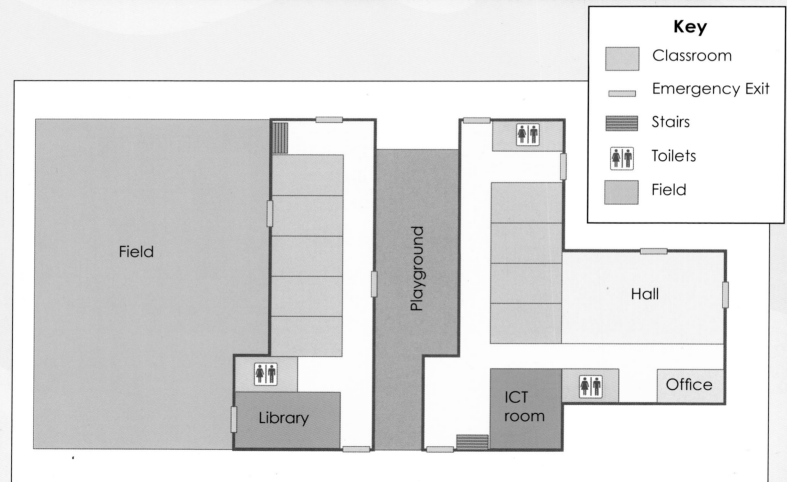

Key

	Classroom
	Emergency Exit
	Stairs
	Toilets
	Field

Field

Playground

Library

Hall

ICT room

Office

This map shows where the buildings, toilets, and office are. It shows pathways. The **labels** help to explain where things are.

Maps show:

⇒ **aerial** views of a place

⇒ where things are

⇒ connections between places, such as paths or roads

⇒ important features.

Street maps

Cities have many buildings and roads, railways lines, and bus stations. Cities have **services** that people need like hospitals, post offices, and schools. They also have play areas like parks, swimming pools, and sports centres.

Street maps show the many features found in a town or city.

Q How can you find the hospital on this street map?

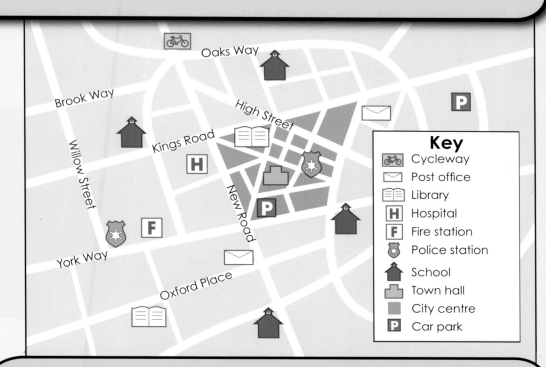

Key
- 🚲 Cycleway
- ✉ Post office
- 📖 Library
- H Hospital
- F Fire station
- 🛡 Police station
- 🏫 School
- 🏛 Town hall
- ▨ City centre
- P Car park

Oaks Way
Brook Way
High Street
Kings Road
Willow Street
New Road
York Way
Oxford Place

? CLUES

- Some features on maps are shown by letters instead of **labels**.

- If P stands for Parking, what letter might be used for a hospital?

 You can find out how the hospital is shown on the map by looking at the **key**. The hospital is marked by the letter H. It can be found on the map between Kings Road and New Road.

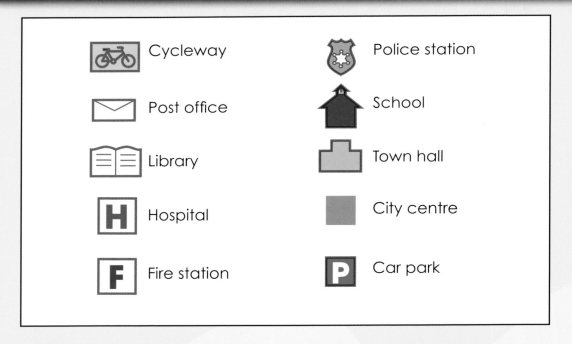

Cycleway		Police station
Post office		School
Library		Town hall
Hospital		City centre
Fire station		Car park

Mapmakers save space by using **symbols** like this to show different features. The symbols can be pictures, shapes, or letters. A map key tells us what the symbols mean.

Transport maps help people find their way round a big, busy city. They show connections between places. This map shows the stops on an underground train route. The different routes are in different colours.

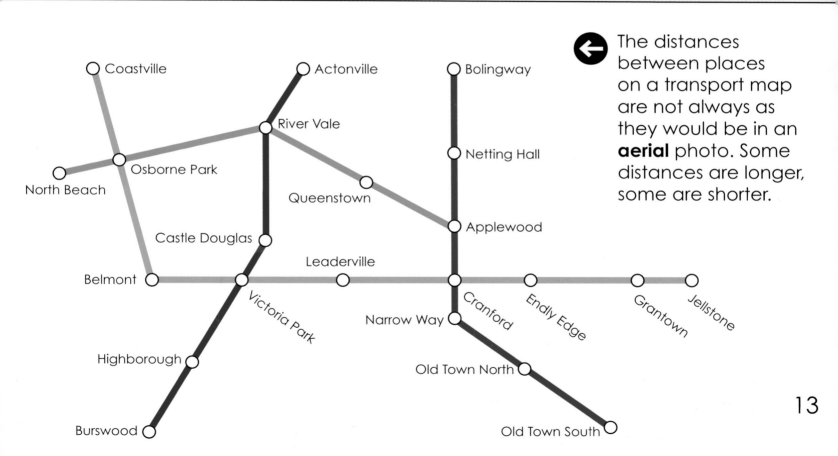

The distances between places on a transport map are not always as they would be in an **aerial** photo. Some distances are longer, some are shorter.

Mapping the land

There are few roads in the countryside. Land maps have to show natural features that are in the country like hills and mountains, woods, rivers, lakes, and fields.

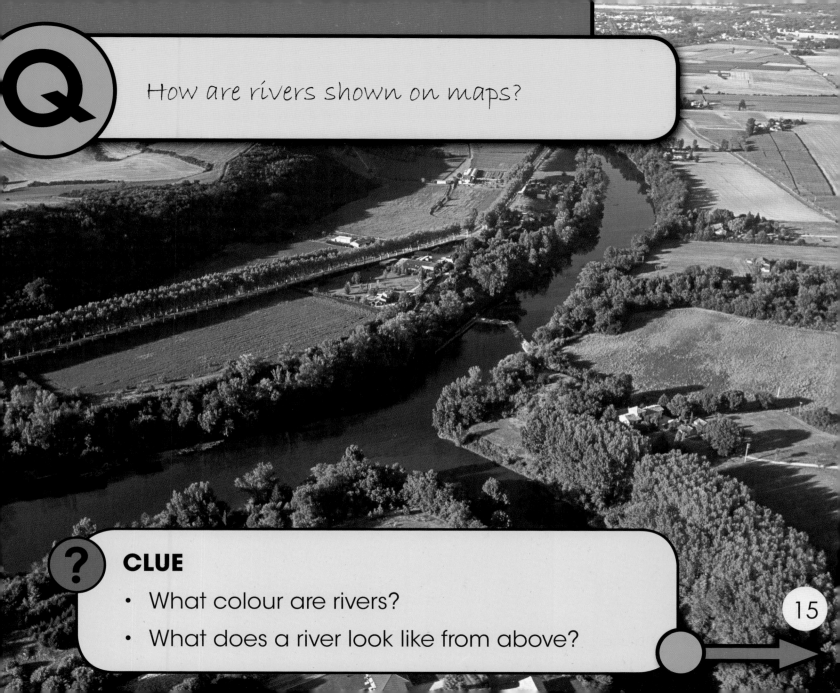

How are rivers shown on maps?

CLUE

- What colour are rivers?
- What does a river look like from above?

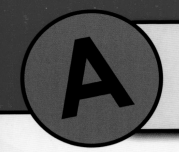

On this map the blue line of the river shows that it flows into a lake. The road crosses the river over Eagle Bridge. The woods are shown by areas of green with little tree **symbols**.

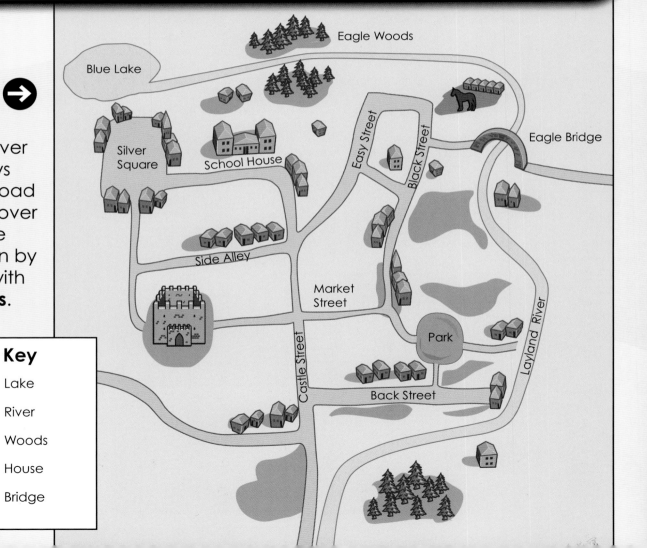

16

Key

	Lake
	River
	Woods
	House
	Bridge

Physical maps use different colours to show different kinds of land. On this map of South America the blue lines are rivers. The blue patches are lakes. High hills and mountains are yellow and white.

World maps

This is a map of the world. It shows the **continents** and oceans. Continents are the world's seven largest **land masses**. Some flat world maps show different features. They may show mountain ranges or capital cities.

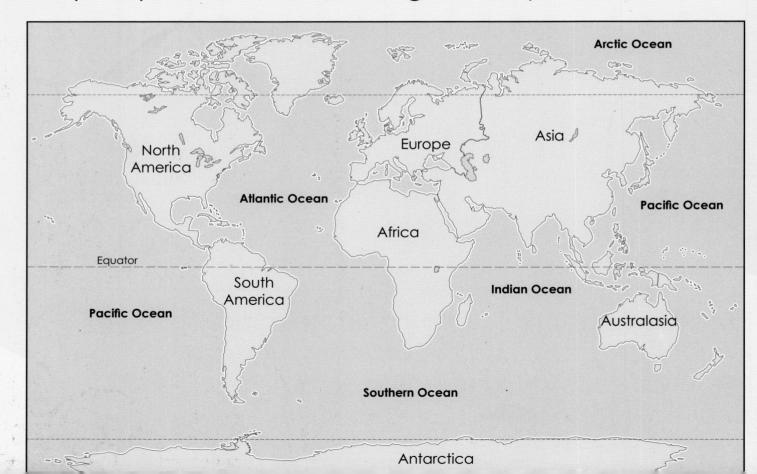

What is the other type of world map we can use?

← This is a photograph of Earth taken from space.

? **CLUE**

- What type of map is the same shape as Earth?

19

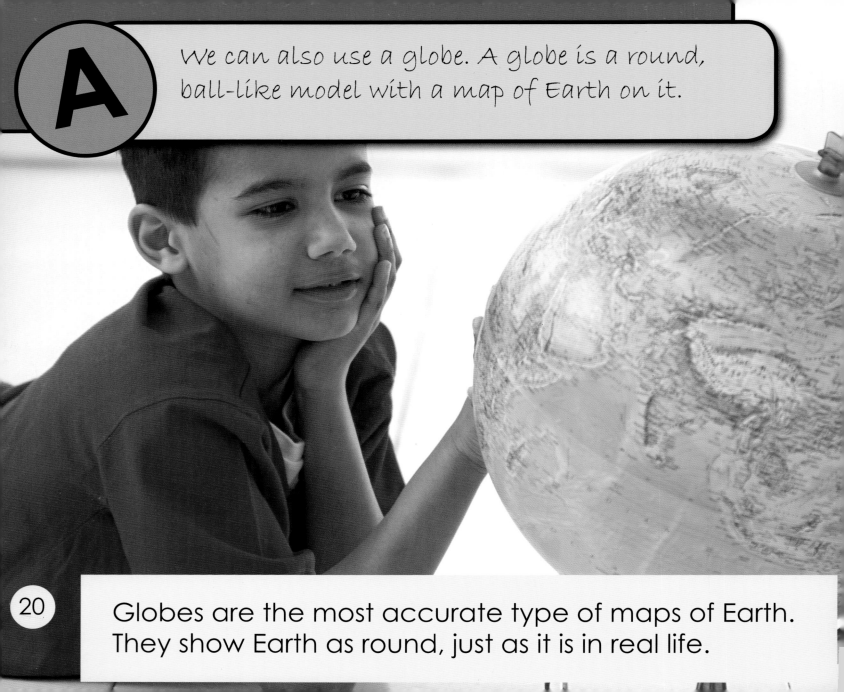

A We can also use a globe. A globe is a round, ball-like model with a map of Earth on it.

Globes are the most accurate type of maps of Earth. They show Earth as round, just as it is in real life.

The North Pole is at the top of the globe. The South Pole is at the opposite end. The Poles are the coldest places on Earth.

North Pole

Equator

South Pole

The Equator is an imaginary line around the middle of a globe. It marks the half-way point between the North and South Poles.

21

Using maps

To use a map there are three other things you need to know:

➠   How to use **compass** points.

➠   How to use a **grid**.

➠   How to work out **scale**.

The needle of a compass always points north. People use a compass to find directions.

Q How do compass points help us use a map?

CLUE

• What can you find on many maps other than a **key**?

Many maps have a **compass symbol** or a **directional arrow**. This helps you to read directions on the map.

You can use north, east, south, and west to follow directions on a map. On this treasure map the treasure is hidden on the south island, just west of the ruins!

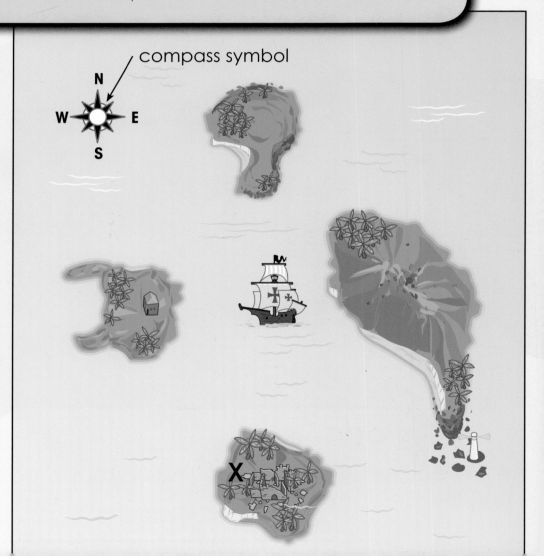

compass symbol

The four directions north, south, east, and west cannot describe exact directions. To give a direction somewhere in between you can say, for example, north-west or south-west.

TIP

You can remember compass directions with a sentence like "Never Eat Slimy Worms". It reminds us of the names of each compass point as you go clockwise round the compass.

Many maps have sets of lines that form **grid** squares. A **grid reference** is the letters or numbers that meet at each square. A grid reference helps us find a place on a map.

→ This treasure map grid has letters going across (horizontally) and numbers going up (vertically). The grid reference for the lighthouse on this map is F,2 and for the hut is B,4.

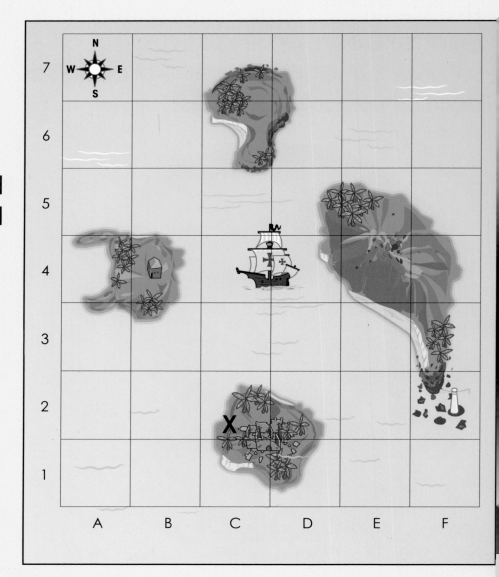

This map has numbers along both sets of grid lines. Grid references for this map are made of four numbers. To find a grid reference first look at the numbers along the bottom of the map. Then go up that grid line to get the next number.

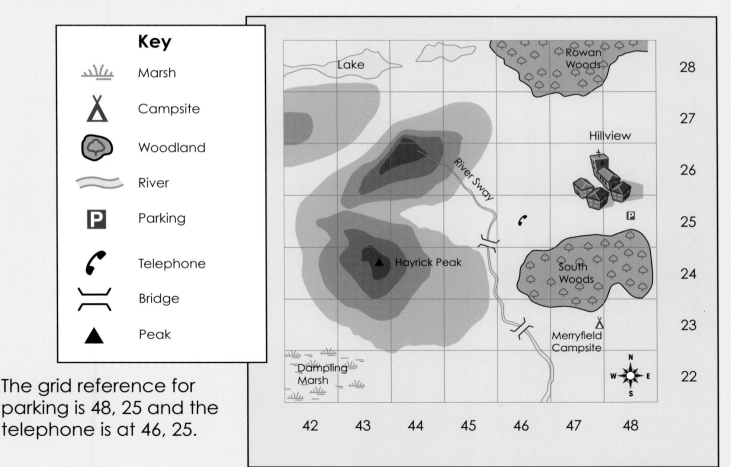

Key

Marsh	
Campsite	
Woodland	
River	
Parking	
Telephone	
Bridge	
Peak	

➡ The grid reference for parking is 48, 25 and the telephone is at 46, 25.

Different maps use different **scales**. The scale bar tells us how much smaller a feature is on the map than it is in real life. For example a scale of 1cm: 2km means that 1cm on the map equals two kilometres on the ground.

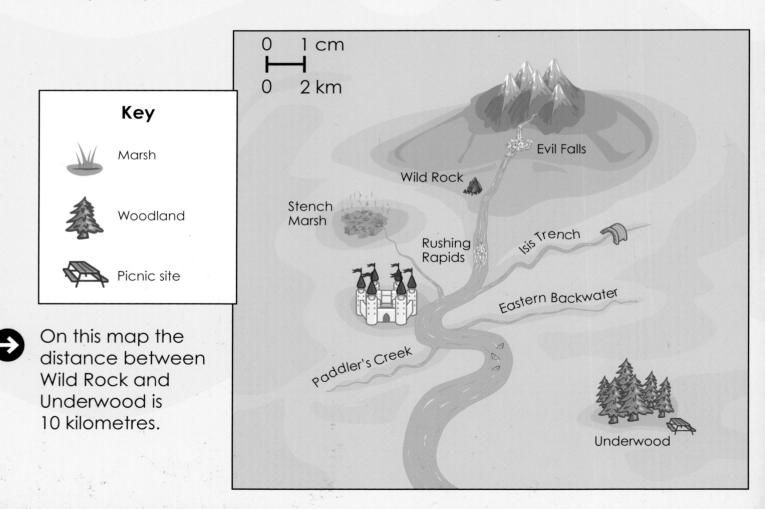

Key

Marsh

Woodland

Picnic site

➡ On this map the distance between Wild Rock and Underwood is 10 kilometres.

Maps are useful for telling us where a place is. Today more and more people use **GPS** systems instead. These electronic gadgets use **satellites** to find your location and guide you to where you want to go. They can show maps on a screen that change as you move.

This GPS system speaks to the driver to tell them which direction to take. The arrow on the map also shows the driver where they need to go.

Checklist

Maps are drawings of places. We use maps to find where things are. There are different kinds of maps, such as:

land maps

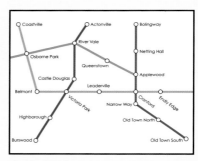
transport maps

plan maps

street maps

world maps

Glossary

aerial overhead, from the sky

compass object with a needle that always points north. People use compasses to help them find directions.

continent one of the seven largest land masses in the world.

directional arrow arrows on a map that show the directions north, south, east, and west. Some directional arrows are drawn to look like a real compass.

GPS GPS is short for Global Positioning System. A GPS gadget gets information from satellites to tell you its exact location on Earth.

grid pattern of lines on a map

grid reference numbers or letters that tell you the location of something on a map that has a grid

key list of words or phrases that explain symbols on a map

label short description that identifies something for a reader

land mass large continuous area of land

permanent something that is always there

satellite object in space that sends out TV signals or takes photographs

scale difference between the size of something in real life and its size on a map

service job or business that supplies people in a settlement with something they need, such as electricity or water

symbol pictures, shapes, or letters that represent objects in real life

Index